Stegosaurus

by Charles Lennie

ABDO
DINOSAURS
Kids

www.abdopublishing.com

Published by Abdo Kids, a division of ABDO, PO Box 398166, Minneapolis, Minnesota 55439.

Copyright © 2015 by Abdo Consulting Group, Inc. International copyrights reserved in all countries. No part of this book may be reproduced in any form without written permission from the publisher.

Printed in the United States of America, North Mankato, Minnesota.

052014

092014

Photo Credits: Getty Images, Minnesota Zoo (mnzoo.org), Shutterstock, Thinkstock, © goran cakmazovic / Shutterstock.com p.5, © Perry Quan / CC-BY-SA-2.0 p.7, © User: HombreDHojalata / CC-BY-SA-3.0 p.9, © Salvatore Frank Vincentz / CC-BY-3.0 p.17

Production Contributors: Teddy Borth, Jennie Forsberg, Grace Hansen

Design Contributors: Candice Keimig, Laura Rask, Dorothy Toth

Library of Congress Control Number: 2013952082

Cataloging-in-Publication Data

Lennie, Charles.

 Stegosaurus / Charles Lennie.

   p. cm. -- (Dinosaurs)

ISBN 978-1-62970-024-3 (lib. bdg.)

Includes bibliographical references and index.

1. Stegosaurus--Juvenile literature.   I. Title.

567.915--dc23

                    2013952082

Table of Contents

Stegosaurus

The Stegosaurus lived

a long time ago. It lived

about 150 million years ago.

4

5

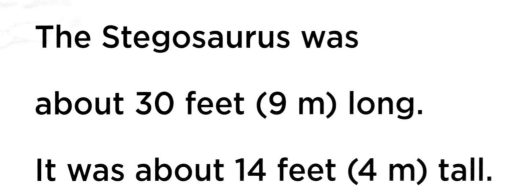

The Stegosaurus was
about 30 feet (9 m) long.

It was about 14 feet (4 m) tall.

The Stegosaurus could

not move very fast. Its

front legs were short.

Its back legs were long.

9

The Stegosaurus had

a short neck. Its head

was low to the ground.

The Stegosaurus had a **beak**.

Its beak tore plants.

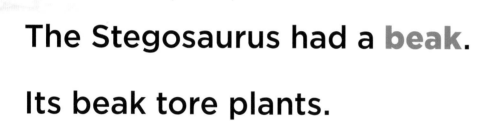

12

The Stegosaurus had plates on its back.

The Stegosaurus also had spikes on its tail. The spikes helped **protect** against **predators**.

Food

The Stegosaurus ate low-lying plants. These plants were easy to reach.

Fossils

Stegosaurus **fossils** have been found all around the world.

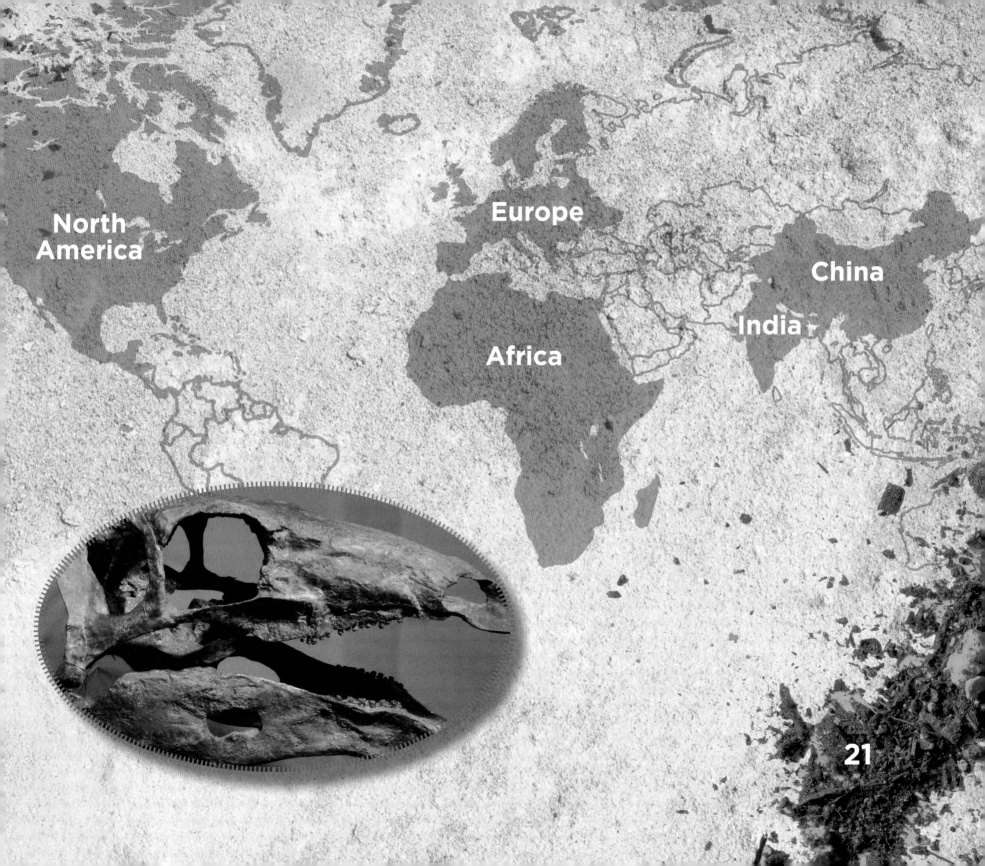

North America

Europe

China

India

Africa

21

More Facts

- The Stegosaurus' brain was small for its size. It was the same size as a dog's, which is the size of a walnut.

- The first Stegosaurus fossil was found in Colorado in 1876.

- Like the Apatosaurus, the Stegosaurus swallowed rocks to help digest its food.

- The Stegosaurus could only move about 5 mph (8.04 km/h).

Glossary

beak – a hard mouthpart that sticks out.

fossil – the remains of a living thing; could
be a footprint or skeleton.

predator – an animal that lives by eating other animals.

protect – to guard against harm or danger.

Index

abdokids.com

Use this code to log on to abdokids.com and access crafts, games, videos and more!

Abdo Kids Code:
DSK0243